The Shamanic Secret Commandment to a Perfect Life

THE MISSING INGREDIENT TO "THE SECRET"

BY MICHAEL WILLIAM DENNEY
www.MichaelWilliamDenney.com

There Is Only One Commandment   3

How I Discovered the Secret Commandment   9

Why Secret "Commandment"?   12

Why "The Secret" Usually Doesn't Work   18

How To Determine Your Deepest Desires   30

When Your Deepest Desires are "Silly"   35

Taking Action On The Secret Commandment   38

Creating Your Perfect Life 41

Unconscious Resistance   44

The Purpose of Unconscious Resistance   54

Conclusion   58

There Is Only One Commandment

In this book, I will share with you the one and only thing you will ever need to accomplish in life. The answer to all of Life's problems is amazingly simple. Everyone can achieve complete fulfillment and mastery in their lives if they follow this one very simple commandment.

The good news is that you have already been pre-wired by the Universe from birth to naturally follow this commandment. So, there is nothing you need to learn. But it is very possible you may have to *unlearn* a few things.

Most of us born in the developed world have been heavily indoctrinated against following this one commandment to living a perfect life. Most of us from birth have been taught to **un**learn our natural ability to follow this one principle which creates our perfect life.

Once I spell out exactly what the one commandment to living your perfect life is, the rest of this book is designed to help you unlearn the incorrect beliefs you have been taught and to reconnect you with your inborn ability to instantly create everything you want in your life.

And, once you understand and accept that following this one commandment will give you absolutely everything in Life and you consciously choose follow it, the Universe will bow down to serve you. Everything in your life will align itself to give you everything you desire.

I know this sounds unbelievable that you can have everything you want, that you can have a perfect life. By "perfect life" I mean exactly that - *perfect*... perfect health, prosperity, happiness, fulfillment, love, excitement and adventure, whatever "perfect" means for you.

Once I began to practice the secret commandment in my own life, everything in my world began to get better and better. It is still continuing to get better and better as I continue to surrender to the idea that I really can have absolutely everything I desire.

When I understood the secret commandment, circumstances began to slowly line up for me in a seemingly magical fashion. I would ask myself, "What do I want in this area of my life?" As long as I was honest about exactly what I wanted and accepted it completely and trusted the Universe to give it to me, it would then appear in my life.

Sometimes my intention would appear immediately or perhaps it took a little while, but it would always appear exactly as I intended it (sometimes even better than I imagined).

So, what is the one and only commandment that you must follow in order to have a perfect life?

The One Commandment to a perfect life is: **Follow Your Deepest Passion**

Really? That's it? "Follow your deepest passion"? Are you kidding me?

I know you have heard this before. But, what you haven't heard is that from the Universe's perspective and from the perspective of your eternal Soul, this is not a suggestion, it is a **command**.

That means that you must obey your inner desires to the letter. You cannot compromise or skimp. This can make some people nervous, but don't worry. You don't have to follow any one else's expectations of you. You only have to follow your own deepest desires. The only problem we encounter in connection to the Secret Commandment is if we stop ourselves from having what we really want in life.

But, you must be honest about what you really want and be willing to take action to fulfill those desires.

We are commanded by our own souls to follow our deepest passions. If we refuse to follow this commandment to follow our deepest passions, we run the risk of experiencing negative consequences. Negative consequences can be things like, emotional issues, (depression, anxiety, fear, anger, etc.,), financial distress and even physical illness.

In order to reap the benefits of this universal commandment, you have to obey your true desires without compromise.

Many people fail in this area of obeying this command to the letter. I know I did for many years. We compromise on our passions. We pursue our passions half-heartedly or we minimize our ideal fantasy life. Or worse yet, we may not even consciously know what our true passions are.

We make deals with ourselves like, "I'll follow my dreams later when I make enough money." Only to discover that the money is never enough and before we know it, we're in our 50's and we still never followed our dreams…

In some cases, people know exactly what their passions are, but they choose to reject pursuing them out of some mistaken belief that their passions are silly, impractical or "wrong" in some other way.

Perhaps their parents shamed them out of following their passion. Perhaps their teachers or religious ministers shamed them out of their passions. For whatever reason, they chose against following their deepest joys in order to gain someone else's approval.

The bad news in these cases is that if we choose against following our deepest passions, we become out of alignment with our own soul and our own inborn destiny. If we choose (whether consciously or unconsciously) to reject our soul's deepest passions, we create an internal conflict within ourselves that will remain unresolved until we consciously choose to follow our deepest joy.

This internal conflict can be very destructive to us on many levels. It is not my intention to create fear, but I have seen in both my own life and in the lives of many others, that when someone is in conflict with themselves about following their deepest passions, they can become unhappy, depressed, and even very physically ill.

This is why I say that the secret commandment is not a suggestion. It is a command. It is your spiritual destiny. If you disobey your internal command, your inborn destiny to live your happiest life, you will, at some point, suffer negative consequences from your choice to deny yourself your dreams.

But, if you choose to obey your soul and follow unreservedly those things that bring you your deepest joys, you can realign yourself with your Soul and have absolutely everything you have ever wanted. You can have your perfect fantasy life, guaranteed.

If making ourselves deliriously happy is the answer to all of our problems, why are so many people miserable? The answer is simple, because of fear. We often fear our own success.

I remember reading somewhere that our biggest fear is not the fear of failure, but the fear of success. For many of us, it is easier to allow ourselves to fail in life in order to save us the disappointment if we fail.

We understand failure, but what will happen to us if we succeed?

So, ask yourself: Are you following your deepest joy or have you compromised on your deepest fantasy?

Most of us have at some point in our lives compromised on what we REALLY want. We go after what we think we

should be doing in life. We accept less in our relationships, our careers, our health, etc.,... Or, we allow ourselves to go after only what we *think* we can realistically expect from life.

We may have doubts that the Universe wants to give us our deepest desires. We may have negative feelings about our deepest passions. This is very normal.

But what if your craziest, most unrealistic fantasy, the thing that you really, truly wish you could have was available to you? Would you take it? You'd be surprised how many people when given the opportunity to have everything they've always wanted, will reject it in favor of something unsatisfying.

But, the good news is that you can always, at any time, no matter how old or young you are, choose to follow your deepest passion and create your ultimate fantasy life.

As simple as this commandment is, to "follow your deepest passion to the letter," I have found, not only through my own experience, but through the experience of others, that implementing the Secret Commandment might be quite confusing and difficult at first.

The problem here lies in a major misconception we have in our modern society. We do not believe we deserve to be truly happy. Many people do not believe that the Universe will grant them their deepest desires. So, they compromise with themselves.

So, even though you may think that you know this secret command already, if you are like me or like most everyone else in the world, you will probably have to change the way you relate to the Universe in order to get the full benefit of your deepest desires.

This is where the shamanic understanding comes in. The shamanic view of reality and your place in the Universe is very different than what you have probably learned from your parents, teachers and ministers. I think I can help you change your thinking about who you are and your role in the Universe.

The remainder of this book is dedicated to helping you change the way you think about yourself and your relationship to the Infinite Universe so that you can instantly and effortlessly align yourself to the Universe in such a way that whatever you desire will instantly begin to manifest for you.

First let me tell you how I found this secret command and how I implemented it in my life.

How I Discovered the Secret Commandment

I discovered the secret commandment to a perfect life for myself during one of the most depressing and difficult periods of my entire life. My desperate circumstances forced me into following the commandment. It started with me going through a sudden and devastating life change.

As a result of my sudden life changes, I had begun following this one commandment to a perfect life without even realizing it. As my old life began to fade away and (seemingly against all odds) this new amazing life began to coalesce for me, I began to ask myself what I had done to create such a wonderful transformation in my life and slowly the answer began to emerge.

What had led up to my understanding of the Secret Commandment came from a very difficult life lesson. I had just gone through a very painful and sudden divorce. I lost everything, my brand new two story house, my martial arts studio, my business, my friends, my dog, my wife, my security,... everything. I was broke and two breaths away from homelessness. I only had my car and whatever I could fit into it. I had no place to go and no idea what I was going to do.

At the time of my divorce from my ex-wife, I was 49 years old and I suddenly found myself living on a friend's couch. I had no idea what I was going to do. I didn't know where I was going to live or how I was going to make a living.

Not only was I going through the emotional devastation of a sudden divorce, I was physically in a HUGE amount of pain. I had joint pain, back pain, crippling muscle spasms, debilitating tendonitis.

I was applying for disability. I had no savings and very little income. I was only making a few hundred dollars a month from book sales. I was looking at the possibility of getting old and I had no way to support myself and I was in way too much pain to work.

Just a few weeks earlier, I was living in a huge, brand new, five bedroom, two story house with an attached studio where I taught martial arts and shamanism. And now, suddenly I was broke, sick, in pain and living on someone's couch.

But, having all of my security blankets suddenly taken away from me gave me a lot of freedom. And that's how I chose to look at it. Even though I had lost all of my material possessions, I had gained total freedom. Since I no longer had to meet the expectations of my wife, my parents, my clients or even my dog, I was completely free to totally reinvent my life from scratch.

How did I want to live? Where did I want to live? What did I want to do?

I did something that had helped me several times in the past. I chose to ignore the seemingly miserable state of my current circumstances and I asked myself, "If I could do anything and live anywhere, what would I do and where would I live?"

One thing on my bucket list was to live in a cabin, deep in the woods away from society and write books and make videos. So, even though I had no money and could not afford it, I used what little credit I had to borrow enough money to put down a first and last month's rent on a cabin deep in the woods of North Idaho.

I found the cabin of my dreams. It was the last cabin on an isolated dirt road 20 miles from the nearest town beneath the Selkirk Mountains situated right on the banks of a rushing river. My property line was the boundary to a national forest. Moose, deer, elk, bald eagles and grizzly bears were my neighbors. It was perfect.

I won't bore you with all the details, but the amazing wilderness setting of that cabin allowed me to begin working furiously on my books and I was able to get started working as a phone counselor. I wasn't making very much money, but somehow I was able to survive and begin rebuilding my life.

Living in that cabin, deep in the woods of Northern Idaho was simultaneously one of the most lonely and yet exciting times of my life. After almost a year, I had sufficiently scratched that itch of living deep in the wilderness by myself. Previously in my life, I had wondered if I belonged living alone in the forest like a hermit. Now, I had fulfilled that long-held desire and I was ready to return to society.

I won't take up space here with all of the amazing experiences I had in that beautiful forest cabin, what is important for you to know is that by fearlessly going after one of my long held dreams, I was unknowingly following the secret commandment and my life began to completely transform.

I was reborn…

Why Secret "Commandment"?

Why am I choosing to use the word "commandment"?

Because that is exactly what it is. It is not optional. The Universe has commanded that we follow this rule. If we choose to reject this commandment, the result can be destructive to our life.

I know it's not popular to command anyone to do anything. It sounds too much like organized religion. But, unlike religion that seeks to coerce you into doing things you don't want, trying to force you to "carry your cross" through life, the Secret Commandment only requires that you do one thing - whatever makes you deliriously happy. But, you must do it to the hilt. If you hold back, you only deprive yourself.

"But, what about other people?" You may ask. *"Aren't I supposed to dedicate my life to the well being of others? If I'm just selfishly focused on my own happiness, won't I be hurting other people?"*

We are all interconnected. If you are empowering yourself, everything else in existence is immediately empowered. If you are harmful to yourself, you will be harming others. So, if what you want is to help other people, the first thing to do is to make yourself happy.

I have seen both in my own life and in the life of others that when people consistently choose to reject implementing this commandment in their lives to follow their deepest desires, they become unhappy and often become very physically sick.

This was true in my case. Even though my divorce was very painful and frightening, it was also the best thing that could have happened to me. Throughout my marriage, I was trying to live according to someone else's expectations of me. I was not happy where I was living and I was not doing what I wanted to do.

I was rejecting the Secret Commandment to live out my deepest passions and fantasies. After a decade of trying to force myself to fit into someone else's mold, besides being very unhappy, I started to become very sick. I gained a lot of weight. I had crippling back pain and muscle spasms. I had debilitating sciatica (pinched nerve in the spinal column). I had a constant swollen and painful knee, I was deeply depressed and I suffered from extremely painful and debilitating tendonitis.

According to doctors, my physical symptoms were a result of sports injuries and martial arts. They told me that there was very little I could do about my pain except learn to manage it through medication and bedrest. They told me I had to limit my physical activities and that I was probably going to have to severely restrict my physical activities for the rest of my life. I was told that I would probably have to rely on pain medication for the rest of my life. (Thankfully, I never listened to that advice!)

Well, I'm here to tell you that all of my physical symptoms disappeared once I started following the Secret Commandment. Even though I was broke, homeless and in pain, I took action as though I was rich and in perfect health. And once I was doing the things I loved again, my body completely healed itself.

Now at 53 years old, I have no joint pain, no knee pain, no back pain, no muscle spasms. I look and feel 30 years younger. According to my recent blood work, I have the health of a 25 year old. At first glance, people often think I am ten or more years younger than I really am.

Now, I am not telling you all of this just to brag. There is an energetic and spiritual science to all of this. The reason my health and life improved so rapidly is because once I started making these changes to my life and fearlessly following my passions, I was allowing the Life Force Energy of the Universe to flow freely to me.

It has nothing to do with making "smart" decisions or being righteous or anything like that. It has to do with making the shift to allow myself to flow with the natural flow of Universal Life Force Energy.

Once you understand the energetic science behind the Secret Commandment, you will understand that anyone can have seemingly eternal youth and joy. It has to do with allowing the Universe to supply you with an Infinite source of Life Force Energy.

Life Force Energy
You may have heard of the words, "chi" or "prana" or "orgone." These are different spiritual terms for the Life Force Energy flowing through the Universe. This Life Force Energy is what gives Life to all things in the Cosmos.

This Life Force Energy is what allows us to live and be healthy. When the flow of Life Force Energy is blocked or constricted, it results in all kinds of problems; illness, sadness, depression, poverty, "bad luck," etc.,...

One of the ways we constrict or block the flow of this Universal Life Force Energy is when we refuse to follow our deepest desires.

When the Universal Life Force Energy is allowed to follow its natural flow in our lives by freely following our deepest desires, we naturally become healthy, happy and prosperous.

In the past, I thought I understood the concept of Life Force Energy. I believed that I could manipulate this Life Force Energy to get what I thought I wanted in life. But, I was frustrated most of the time. What I have learned since that time is that we cannot manipulate this Energy, we have to obey it and flow with it. We obey it by following our natural desires.

When we flow with this Infinite Life Force Energy, the Universe bows down before us and gives us everything we need. And by "everything", I mean EVERYTHING; money, health, romance, happiness, youth, luck, everything you can imagine will be at your fingertips. All you need to do is think about what you want and need and it will magically come to you.

Some of you may have resistance to the idea of obeying anything. It sounds very religious. I understand your caution here. I too, do not like the idea of obedience in a religious way.

But, when it comes to obeying the Life Force Energy in the Universe, it is VERY different than obeying an external force like a judgmental god who sits in the heavens and commands you to do things you do not like to do.

In fact, it is important to understand that in order for us to obey the Secret Commandment, we may need to change the way we see the Universe.

According to the Secret Commandment, YOU are the one who controls the Universe. It is YOU whom you must obey. This is in direct opposition to most religious teachings that tell you that you must deny yourself and bow down before an angry god and obey him.

The Secret Commandment says that you must obey YOUR deepest desires, YOUR deepest passions. It is not some god in the heavens whom you must obey, it is YOU.

And here is the best part, when you listen to your own wishes and obey them, God (whatever that means to you) must bow down to you to obey and serve you.

When someone obeys their deepest desires, they automatically sit on the throne of Heaven and create the entire Universe.

The Universe obeys you and bows down to you when you fearlessly follow your deepest desires.

If you have resistance to this view of God, I understand. Perhaps another way to view it is that God has commanded you to follow his Will. And his will for you is embedded in your deepest desires. The way God shows you his will for you is by implanting desires in you that will bring you your deepest joy.

However you choose to look at it, the result is the same. If you reject your deepest desires, you will be unhappy. If you follow your deepest desires, you will master your life.

Why "The Secret" Usually Doesn't Work

Most likely, you are familiar with new age teaching best known as "The Secret" which teaches that you can manifest whatever you focus on. This is absolutely correct but it is incomplete.

From the perspective of the Secret Commandment, when you are obeying your deepest desires and focusing your intentions on how to fulfill those desires, whatever you focus on magically manifests for you.

So, the Secret Commandment and the "Secret" are in perfect alignment here. But, often times people who try to use "the Secret" often operate from a faulty and incomplete assumption about how manifestation works.

The faulty assumption associated with "the Secret" is the assumption is that you can manifest *whatever* you focus on. If this were true, everyone would be a billionaire.

Since most people believe that if they were rich, they would be happy, money is what most people focus their intentions on. And rarely is someone satisfied with their amount of money. The more you get, the more you want.

So, the foundation of "the secret" is incomplete. It assumes that you can arbitrarily decide what you want. And often times, people mistakenly focus on manifesting things based on their fears, things they don't really want on a Soul level.

So, they focus on cars or boats or something that represents to their fears as something of value. But, your Soul does not recognize these things as valuable. So, there is an inherent conflict.

And when you are in conflict with yourself, you run the risk of giving conflicting signals to the Universe, so you will most likely get conflicting results.

When people focus on things they *think* they need based on their fears, (usually material things), they are out of alignment with their Soul. But, the Soul does not operate from fear and rarely needs material things.

So, part of this process is to listen to your Soul rather than your fears. This may cause some conflict and confusion. But that is part of the fun - to figure what your Soul really wants.

Your Soul will only focus on activities and lifestyles that bring you great joy. So, if your desires require money, (often times you can get these things with little or no money), instead of focusing on the money you think you need, just focus on the activity or the lifestyle and assume you will have whatever money you need to achieve it. Don't worry about the dollar amount. The Universe will figure that out for you.

The Secret works only if one understands that the Universe instantly manifests our deepest desires when we focus on them and take action to fulfill them. But, if a person focuses on something that they only THINK they want, they usually fail to manifest their intentions or worse yet are unsatisfied if they do manifest their intentions.

Where most people incorrectly apply the Secret is when they try to focus on manifesting things that are not in alignment with their deepest desires. Often times, people are confused about what they really want as opposed to what they THINK they want.

We can lie to ourselves, but the Universe cannot be fooled. If you focus on something that you only THINK you want or on something that you have been taught to believe you want or what you believe you SHOULD want, you will be in conflict with your deepest awareness.

The Universe picks up on your internal conflict and manifests with varying results.

You see, most people do not believe that the Universe WANTS them to have their deepest desires fulfilled. Most people do not trust the Universe to naturally fulfill their passions and desires and so they think they have to get it for themselves.

So, they use "the secret" as a way to "cheat" and get what they think they want from the Universe. Most people are not doing this on a conscious level. This is usually happening on an unconscious level. They unconsciously believe that they are unworthy of their deepest desires.

They unconsciously feel guilty about what they really want and so they are in deep conflict. They unconsciously believe that the Universe is against them. This creates fear and insecurity and their intentions become laced with fear.

The result of this conflicted focus is that the Universe gets double messages from them about what they want to manifest and as a result, they get mixed results from their intentions.

This belief that they are not worthy of their deepest desires comes from the pervasive false religious teachings we discussed in the previous chapter.

Most of us have been subtly and repeatedly indoctrinated by our government, our society, our teachers, our ministers, etc.,… to believe that the Universe is an empty, cold, cruel place that is constantly seeking to harm us and deny us our passions.

This false belief is from a very old religious belief system that was put into place in our society during the Middle Ages, hundreds of years ago. Even though most of us, on a conscious level, reject these outdated beliefs, nevertheless, we still carry these toxic beliefs deep in our unconscious minds and they still have a profound effect on our thoughts and feelings.

As a result, even if someone is a progressive thinking, spiritual person, they may still believe on a deep unconscious level, that they need to protect themselves from the cold, cruel universe by surrounding themselves with a lot of material things like money, houses, cars etc.,…

So, because they believe that they must provide themselves with all their resources, they first focus on manifesting money, cars, houses, fame, etc.,… And even if they are successful in getting these things, (most people are unsuccessful in this area of manifesting) they still find that they are lonely, scared and unhappy.

If, like most people, they are unsuccessful in manifesting the money and the cars and the houses that they think they want, they then assume that the Secret is false and they give up. Or worse, they assume that they are doing something wrong and they judge themselves for being "bad" at manifesting.

They may continue to try even harder and harder to believe in "the Secret" for years with little or no success. This only creates a deeper sense of fear, frustration and insecurity. This negative cycle creates a self-fulfilling prophecy of failure and you can guess the rest of the story…

So, this brings us to another fundamental rule regarding the Secret Commandment:

Successful manifesting of desires is based on Trust...

The Universe does not manifest intentions based in fear or insecurity. If people are focusing on manifesting out of fear or insecurity, the Universe only sees the fear and manifests according to their insecurity. Even if they are focusing on money, for example, if the desire for money comes from fear of lack, they usually only manifest lack, not money.

If someone believes that they must first manifest lots of money or material possessions in order to follow their deepest passions, they are operating from a false assumption that the Universe is against them and they feel they need to surround themselves with material things to protect them from the very Universe that is seeking to bring them joy.

I run into this almost every day in my phone consultations. When I encourage someone to fearlessly follow their passions, a client will often say, "I would love to, but first I need to make enough money so that I don't have to work. When I have enough money to not work, then I can follow my dreams."

To which I respond that the Universe does not work that way. First you must focus on your deepest desires and imagine yourself living that dream regardless of money. If you focus on your innate fantasies and take action towards them, the Universe will provide any money *if it is needed*.

The Universe has no interest in manifesting money or resources you don't need to fulfill your Soul Desire. The

Universe does not like to waste energy. If deep in your Soul you know that you only need $40,000 a year to fulfill all of your desires, the Universe is not going to give you $100,000 per year just to feed your insecurity.

Think about it. How much do you REALLY need to achieve all of your true desires? I know from personal experience that it doesn't necessarily take a lot of money to have abundance in all areas. You also know this on a deep level. So, focus on what you really want and just allow the Universe to provide what you need to accomplish it.

If you are not manifesting as much money as you think you need, then either you are in conflict with yourself about how much money you really need in order to accomplish your Soul Desire, OR, you may be operating from a place of fear and insecurity.

You see, the Universe does not recognize money by itself as anything of value. The Universe only recognizes practical manifestations of resources. Money is only one form of resources.

Money is nothing more than a symbol of physical resources. Money, by itself, cannot feed or clothe you. It cannot love you or keep you warm at night. The only way money has any use is if two parties agree to accept that symbol of money in exchange for whatever practical resource you need.

The Universe provides whatever resource is necessary for you to fulfill your deepest desires. And you would be surprised at how little money you may need to live your wildest dreams.

That is why focusing on money alone is a waste of time, because the Universe does not recognize empty symbols.

For example, let's imagine someone whose dream is to live in the wilderness and spend time enjoying their passion of being isolated in pristine forest wilderness. Many people might think that in order to afford this lifestyle, a person would need to be extremely wealthy in order to buy a huge parcel of land in the Rocky Mountains, build a multimillion dollar mansion where they can be isolated in the forest.

But, if the individual forgets about how much money they think they need to accomplish their dream and instead fantasizes about simply being in pristine wilderness, they may end up manifesting a career which provides them with their fantasy life, such as a forest ranger.

I remember backpacking deep in the Sierra Nevada Mountains and meeting backcountry rangers who lived in backcountry ranger stations miles away from anything in the most beautiful, isolated locations imaginable. One would have to hike for days to get to these places.

These backcountry ranger stations were beautiful, comfortable cabins located in the middle of the most pristine wilderness you've ever seen. One in particular was at 10,000 feet over 25 miles deep into the backcountry. To get to these cabins, one would have to hike over two mountain passes over 14,000 feet. It would take the average person three days to get to this cabin. Situated on an alpine lake surrounded by majestic granite peaks, this was the premiere mountain getaway.

The government provided these people with the premiere wilderness cabins to live in for free and then paid them a salary on top of that. These rangers worked a few hours a day, patrolling the wilderness on horseback (provided by the gov't.), they helped any hikers they met and answered questions and then when their day of "work" was over, they could do anything they wanted, hike, fish, sleep… whatever… And they got *paid* to do it!

Assuming their fantasy was to live in the wilderness, they got the most exclusive wilderness homes given to them at no cost. The cabins they lived in were in such amazing wilderness locations and no one, no matter how rich would be able to buy them.

Point being, that money does not always buy you anything you want. But, your inner desires can get you absolutely the best of everything that is in accordance with your deepest desires.

If you are only focused on empty symbols alone like money, you may be actually confusing the Universe which only focuses on real energetic resources.

You see, money is only the symbolic expression of energy. Just like clothes, shelter, happiness, health, love, food, etc.,… The universe does not differentiate between different types of energy resources. The Universe only sees different manifestations of energy.

The Universe does not know the difference between the energy to provide resources (money) and the energy to provide a healthy body and mind. Do you know of any rich people who are sick? Of course you do. Do you know of any "poor" people who are healthy and happy? Of course you do...

If someone is a billionaire but doesn't have enough Life Force Energy to keep them physically healthy, their money is completely useless to them. In many cases, the stress that is needed to obtain and keep their money is the direct cause for their illness.

I recently heard a phrase that exemplifies this: *"Some people are so poor, all they have is money."*

Money is only a form of Life Force Energy and, as a rule, the Universe does not give more Energy than is needed to help you fulfill your deepest desires. If money is something that is necessary for the Universe to provide to help you achieve your deepest passions, the money will be there.

If your deepest desire is to live on the beach and surf all day, then maybe all you need is enough money to rent a small apartment and buy a couple of surfboards. In either case, each person, if they are fulfilling their deepest passions will feel, in their own way, like the richest person in the world.

If on the other hand, the billionaire constantly working, with no free time that is stressed out and worried about how to pay his gigantic mortgage and protect his stocks and investments and has no time to enjoy his money, he will feel like a pauper. If he is physically unwell, then he will really feel poor.

As a rule, from the shamanic perspective, if someone is suffering from chronic ill health, that is often a sign that they are not in alignment with their deepest desires and no amount of money, medicines or doctors will cure them. The only thing that will heal them is for them to operate from their soul, from their deepest desires.

But, the "poor" guy who lives on the beach and surfs all day is probably going to be in great physical health and most likely will be very happy if that is what he passionately wants from his life. This is why "poor" people can be in great health and rich people can be on death's door.

In fact, I recently heard of a friend's father who had been suffering from Parkinson's disease. He was taking all kinds of medication for this disease. He recently began focusing on following his desires. He found love in a new relationship and focused more time and energy on having fun and enjoying life. Guess what? His Parkinson's symptoms disappeared and he was able to wean himself off of his medication. His doctor has now declared that he no longer has Parkinson's.

Let me give you an example in my own life. When I got divorced and moved back to Southern California, I had very little money, but I had more than enough money to completely fulfill my deepest desires and as a result, I felt like the richest, luckiest man on the planet.

For a time, after leaving Idaho, I lived in the local Southern California Mountains renting a small cabin. Right outside my door was a wilderness hiking trail that I trekked on every day for hours at a time. Even though I was not "rich," I had enough money to work for myself on my own schedule.

If I didn't think about how much money I did or didn't have, I was ecstatic. I had learned that if I follow my passions, the Universe will ALWAYS give me everything I need to be happy.

I knew of expensive, crowded, noisy neighborhoods in Los Angeles that contained multi-million dollar houses that did not have access to the wilderness. In my little mountain cabin, on the other hand, I had almost no neighbors and I had thousands of acres of pristine wilderness right outside my front door and a view that surpassed most of the views of the mansions in Los Angeles.

I had total freedom, health, peace and happiness. No amount of money could buy that. I was the richest man on the planet. I was doing exactly what I wanted to do.

I am quite sure that many of the owners of those million dollar mansions in the suburbs had a lot less free time to enjoy their money. I bet that most of them are working their tails off so that someday they can follow their passions once they retire.

Speaking for myself, I am not going to wait until I'm too old to enjoy my life. I want to live it to the fullest right now!

Do you see where I'm going? Even though I was "poor" according to my bank account balance, I was enjoying the life of a king. Money had little to do with it all.
I committed myself to following my deepest passions and as a result, the Universe provided me with the resources necessary to live in my version of Nirvana.

So, the first step to manifesting your deepest desires is to first accept that the Universe WANTS to make you happy and the second step is simply accept that Universe MUST obey your deepest desires.

Your only requirement is to take direct action toward your deepest desires regardless of your current circumstances. The Universe will spring into action once you do so and supply you with whatever resources you may need to reach your dreams.

How To Determine Your Deepest Desires

Some of you reading this book may already know what your deepest desires are. Some of you may THINK you know what your deepest desires are and some of you may be confused about what you really want.

So, before we go any further, I will teach you a very easy and powerful method to discover what your deepest desires are in life.

In one of my first books, "Wealth Shaman" I teach a shamanic meditation to determine your deepest desires.

For those wishing to learn a more shamanic approach to this technique, I recommend you get that book and follow the exercises in that book.

But for now, I will teach you an extremely simple but no less powerful method to instantly determine your deepest desires. It starts with pretending.

Pretending means that you forget the rules of reality and allow yourself to fantasize just like little kids do. For this part of the technique, we are going to pretend that there are no rules and that ANYTHING can happen.

So, take a deep breath and say to yourself, "Let's play pretend."

OK, so now we are playing pretend and anything is possible. In your pretend world, anyone can do anything they want and be anything they want. You do not have to worry about money and you don't have to work for a living. The Universe instantly provides you with anything you want at any time.

So, in your pretend world, where you can be and do anything you want where you don't have to work and you don't need any money, what would you do?

Remember that we are playing pretend here, so if you want to be a superhero, you can be that. So do not limit yourself. No matter how unrealistic or unbelievable your fantasy feels, allow yourself to go there.

Now, take a look at your fantasy. What are you doing in your fantasy world?

Well, whatever you are doing in your fantasy is what you are meant to do in the "real" world.

Again, for some people, this may sound unrealistic. But whatever fantasy gives you the greatest joy is what you are meant to do. It is the commandment the Universe has given you. And if you follow that commandment, all of Infinity will serve you.

Now that you know what it is, your job is to take action to make that fantasy a reality.

Here is where many people get stuck. They can indulge in the fantasy, but when it comes to taking action to achieve it, they compromise.

The one aspect from our fantasy that we must bring back into "reality" is that the Universe WANTS to provide us with everything we need to fulfill our fantasy life. But, in order for that to happen we have to believe that the Universe will help us.

In order for anything to come to us, we first have to take action to achieve it. For many, they stop short here. They may not believe that the Universe will help them achieve what they want. In order to take action, they need some kind of "proof" that the Universe wants to help them achieve their fantasies.

This is why so many people want to win the lottery. They believe that if they get a ton of money dropped in their lap, that they can take action on their dreams. But this is not how the Universe works when it comes to manifesting our desires.

I hear this all the time in my counseling work. When I help a person discover their Soul Desire and encourage them to take action to fulfill it, they often tell me, "Well, I can't take action yet, I need to make more money first."

This is how people stay stuck and never move forward. This is because the feeling that you need to make more money before you can take action toward your dream comes from a place of insecurity. It means that you do not believe the Universe will provide you with the resources necessary to fulfill your dreams.

So, while you are waiting to make more money or win the lottery, the Universe is waiting for you to take action. The Universe has all of the money and resources necessary for your Soul Desire and is impatiently waiting to give it to you, but you need to take action first. Taking action is how you give the Universe **permission** to provide you with what you need.

If you are waiting for money before you take action, that is like saying to the Universe, "Wait, I'm not ready yet." And the Universe withholds resources from you because you are giving it the message that you do not want the resources yet.

The Universe honors your fantasies but only responds to action. Taking action is how you show the Universe that you are serious and that you trust that Universe will provide for you. You can be as scared as you want, you can be full of disbelief, as long as you take direct action.

The Universe responds to your action more than your feelings. So, take action!

Remember that the Universe is here to SERVE us, not the other way around. The Infinite Universe is waiting for you to take action toward what you want, THEN it responds by supplying the necessary resources to fulfill that desire.

It is a Universal Shamanic rule that in order to allow the Universe to release the resources necessary to achieve our fantasies, we first have to take action toward them.

The shamanic understanding is exactly like our pretend world. Everything you need will be given to you once you surrender to your dreams, believe that the Universe will support you in manifesting your deepest desires and you take action to create them.

Let me give you another example. Let's say your dream is to become a champion body builder.

Waiting for the Universe to make you rich before you take action on your dream is like sitting at home and saying, "I want to be the next world champion body builder but I'm going to sit here at home and wait for my muscles to grow and then I'll know it's time to go to the gym and work out."

That's ridiculous, right? You don't have to wait to get in shape. Your body is ready to build muscle right now. But it can't do so until you get off your butt and go to the gym. Your muscles will respond the moment you start pushing that weight and not a moment before.

Once you take action and go to the gym and start lifting those weights, THEN your body IMMEDIATELY starts taking protein from your body and your food and begins building muscle.

And every day that you go to the gym, while you sleep, your body is actively building muscle for you, taking the nutrients it needs for that day to create your new muscular physique.

This is how the Universe provides for you when you take action on your Soul Desire. You will get what you need for that day. The more action you take, the more resources you will be given. This is how the Universe works to help you create your perfect life.

When Your Deepest Desires are "Silly"

When working with clients to help them find their Soul Desire, often times after they have imagined their fantasy reality, they may say, *"I can't do that. That's silly."*

Many of us have been indoctrinated to believe that whatever it is we are supposed to do with our lives must be practical or important or valuable to society, etc.,... and if we enjoy something, it is probably a selfish waste of time.

I remember meeting a man, let's say his name is Fred, who was struggling with his realty business. I was working a part time job with him. We both needed extra money.

While working side by side with him, I listened to him complain for hours about how he had to find ways to make more money because he had to keep his two story house. The housing market was a bust and he had all these bills, etc., etc.,…

After asking him a few questions, I came to learn that he had become a realtor because his father was a successful realtor and he was trying (at age 49) to gain his Dad's approval by being a successful realtor like his Dad.

He complained about how many hours he spent showing properties and making no sales. Hours and hours of "taxes this and the government that and the housing market slow down, blah, blah…"

So, I asked him if he didn't have to worry about money and having to work his job, what would he do. *"What do you mean?"* He said. *"What is your favorite hobby?"* I asked.

He told me that he enjoyed taking long distance bicycle rides. I asked him, *"What would be a good way to turn that into a business?"* He said, *"It would be fun to live in the mountains and organize long-distance bike rides for people or groups of people."* *"Well, there you go!"* I exclaimed. *"Now, you know what you should be doing for a living."*

"Oh, no. I can't do that. I have to get myself out of debt." Then I heard the voice of his father come through, *"I can't just waste my time in frivolous hobbies. I have to work a real job. I have to make repairs on this house."* (He lived alone in a two story, four bedroom house in the suburbs) *I'm too lazy. I need to get my life together... I need to invest in my savings for my retirement..."*

"Why don't you just sell the house, take a loss, move to a little cabin in the mountains and begin advertising bike packages for tourists? People would eat it up!"

"No, you don't understand. I can't just leave this job. I have responsibilities,..." and he went on and on again. So, I gave up trying to talk him out of his misery.

The thing is, Fred was miserable. He was horrible at his job because he hated doing it. He resented his father, yet was trying so hard to please him.

It's easy for me to see what he really wants to do, but until he is ready to live for himself, there is nothing anyone else can say to Fred.

But listening to Fred complain about his life really woke me up, once again, to realize that I only have this one life in this body and wasting time trying to please other people is, well... a complete waste of time.

The real reason Fred was a failure as a realtor wasn't because he was bad at it. It's because, selling houses wasn't what he really wanted to do. Fred wanted to spend his life riding bicycles.

Fred grew up with a critical father who downplayed his dream of being a bicycle racer and now, even at age 49, Fred was not able to "get his life together" and be the "responsible" person his father always wanted him to be. He was still stuck in the past, hoping his aging father would suddenly praise him and accept him as a good boy.

I'm not trying to make light of Fred's problem. I understand what he was going through. I remember the last thing I said to Fred about this issue, *"Y'know, when this life is over, you are not going to look back at how much money you made or how 'responsible' you were. You are going to ask yourself if you enjoyed your life."*

Taking Action On The Secret Commandment

OK, so now you most likely have an idea of what your deepest desire is. Hopefully, you have made a commitment to fulfilling that desire. But, taking action on it may seem daunting.

Once again, I want to emphasize that even if you don't think you have the resources to take action on your desires, that is exactly what you have to do in order to reap the benefits of the Secret Commandment.

The Universe is made up of Energy. Money is an arbitrary human invention. Energy is potential not literal. For example, there is enough potential energy in the nucleus of an atom to destroy the world. But in order to activate the energy, we have to unlock its potential.

You are surrounded by unlimited amounts of potential energy and resources, we just have to activate that potential. ACTION, activates potential.

This is why the Universe doesn't know from money. It only knows about energy and resources. Until you take action to fulfill your desire, the Universe does not see the need to release the potential resources to fulfill your desire.

Thinking about living your dream and taking action to make your dream come true are two different things. So, waiting around for the money to appear is a waste of time. Take action toward your dream and the resources you need (which may not be money) will appear.

Actually, it is your own subconscious mind that releases energy to create your dream. But, your subconscious needs to know you are serious about your desires. The only way to notify your subconscious to manifest your desires is when you take action. When you take action that you cannot take back, that is seen by your subconscious mind as a command to create your dream.

Imagine your boss wants you to take a business trip. The trip will be paid for by your employer. But first, you need to get the itinerary to your boss before he can sign off on the trip expenses.

Imagine that he says, *"Once you get to the airport and buy your ticket, text me the airline and the flight # and I'll deposit the funds into your bank account."* If you do not buy the ticket, your boss can't reimburse you.

That is similar to how the Universe works when it comes to fulfilling your desires. Once you take direct and real action to fulfill your desire, the Universe takes notice and releases any energy and resources needed to support and manifest your desires.

The more bold the action, the more likely you are to get a strong reaction from the Universe to support your dream.

In the previous example, I suggested to Fred that he sell his house for a loss and move to the mountains. That would have been a very clear sign to the Universe that Fred was serious about living his dream. Because once he sold his house, he would not be able to turn back. So, you need to take actions that irreversibly commit you to your dreams.

How many times have you heard stories of people taking risks to live their dream? Someone moves to New York to become a dancer or a stage actor. They arrive with no money, not knowing how they will survive, yet somehow circumstances "magically" line up to help them survive and reach their goals.

So, once again, it is important that we realize that we don't have to win the lottery before we can take action to live our dreams. Taking risks is the proof that we trust the Universe to support us. Realizing that the Universe is not only supportive of our dreams, it NEEDS our dreams like we need food, water and air.

Living our dreams is what gives life to the Universe.

Creating Your Perfect Life

OK, so you have a good foundation of how the Secret Commandment works, now we go into action to create our perfect life.

Step 1 - Ask yourself, if you lived in a magical fantasy world where you can be and do anything, what would your life look like? Where would you live? What would you be doing to make yourself happy? What would your personal relationships look like? Are you single, married, do you have children? etc.,…

Step 2 - Examine your chosen new life. Is this really what you want or are you compromising? Remember that in order to reap the most out of the Secret Commandment, you need to create your deepest desires to the full. So, ask yourself if you are going after what you really, really want or are you skimping in order to be more 'practical' or 'sensible.'

This is your one and only life in this body. You have a responsibility to yourself to have as much fun as is humanly possible. If you hold back on making yourself happy, you run the risk of holding a secret grudge against yourself for not going after your greatest joy in life.

Step 3 - Begin taking action to fulfill your desire no matter how impossible it may seem. Let's say you work at Walmart as a greeter, but you imagine yourself living on a yacht in the Mediterranean. You can take action to fulfill this dream by looking at different yachts. Don't look at the price. Look at what will meet your needs. Begin researching where in the Mediterranean you would live. Enjoy imagining what that would feel like.

As another example, imagine someone who lives in the Midwestern United States but fantasizes about living in a tropical paradise like Florida or Hawaii. In that case begin researching different places you might want to live. If you can afford it, take a couple of trips to these destinations to decide where exactly you might move to.

These are just a couple of examples. The point here is that taking action can be as simple as fantasizing but can include taking action to make it happen.

Step 4 - Continue to take action every day. When you experience fear or procrastination, ask yourself what you are afraid of. Write down your fears and feelings around the issue.

Keep Yourself Open to Unorthodox Possibilities
The Universe is economical in how it provides resources. So, don't limit the Universe in how it will manifest your resources. This is where people can get stuck. People know that they need money to accomplish an objective and they automatically assume there is only one way to accomplish that, for example, "I have to win the lottery" etc.,…

The Universe also will respect your boundaries. If you are very attached to the idea that the only way to get what you want is by winning the lottery, the Universe will respect that. That doesn't mean you will win the lottery. It means that the Universe will not provide alternative means because you have already decided that other possibilities are off the table.

To illustrate this, imagine that you have a very savvy accountant working for you and he has come up with a brilliant way to get grants from the gov't. and it could make you a millionaire.

He comes to you with his genius hair-brained scheme and you say, "No. That won't work. I have to win the lottery." The accountant shrugs his shoulders and walks away. He's ready to pull the trigger on a radically different approach that no one has ever thought of but he can't implement it because you won't trust him to do something unorthodox.

In my experience, the Universe is always looking for the quickest way to achieve what you need. I'll share another example from my life. At one point, I had decided that I needed $10,000 to pay off debts. I also wanted to get a new car with better gas mileage to save money for my surf excursions. I meditated and sent out the request, more like a demand, for the Universe to bring me $10,000.

Here's what happened. I got into a car accident and totaled my Jeep. I had bought this jeep used in Idaho on a trade-in for no money. It was just a straight across trade because my pick up was worth more in Idaho than the Jeep was that I wanted. Even though the Jeep was in better condition and was newer with fewer miles than my pick up.

When I moved to California, the Jeep I had was worth more because Californians like Jeeps more than they do pick ups. So, when I totaled my Jeep, the insurance company gave me more money for my totaled Jeep than it was worth when I bought it in Idaho.

The insurance company gave me over $10,000 for my totaled Jeep. I kept the ten grand and used it to pay off some debts and used what was left over to put a down payment on a new car.

So, in essence, I got the $10,000 I needed plus a free upgrade to a new car, all this from a car accident. This is how the Universe works sometimes. It looks for the quickest and easiest way to get you what you need but it may come in ways you don't expect.

Once again, the bottom line is to determine what you want and then take action so that the Universe can release the resources necessary to grant your desires.

Unconscious Resistance

Now, I must be honest with you. If you are making a big change in your life in order to fulfill your deepest desires, there is a very strong likelihood that you will experience strong resistance from your unconscious fears. These unconscious fears will do everything in their power to prevent you from breaking free from your old patterns.

You must become vigilant in seeking to become aware of the subtle power of your unconscious mind and its sneaky tactics to sabotage your success.

Often times, after someone has taken risks to fulfill their desires, unconscious resistance will kick in and can destroy one's progress toward living their desires.

In tragic cases, unconscious resistance can force a person to discard their progress and return to their previous state of unhappiness.

Before I give examples of how resistance can manifest, let me explain what unconscious resistance is and why it can be so difficult to identify and overcome.

The Three Minds
You have three separate minds at play here. You have your conscious mind, your subconscious mind and your unconscious mind.

Your conscious mind is what you are consciously aware of. It is our waking mind. The conscious mind is our interface with moment to moment waking reality.

Your subconscious mind, among other things, is the repository for valuable information that you may need at a moment's notice. For example, your pin numbers, address, your spouse's birthday (hopefully) are stored in your subconscious mind at the ready in case your conscious mind needs access to this information.

Your unconscious mind is the vast storehouse of deep memories, fears, psychological patterns that determine your choices and actions.

The conscious mind is the tip of the iceberg floating above the water's surface.

The subconscious mind is right at the water level line, bobbing above and below the surface as needed.

The unconscious mind is the remaining 85% of you that remains hidden from view but which determines all of your actions and reactions.

So, it is virtually inescapable that when you take drastic action to shift your life away from old patterns and move toward fulfilling your deepest desires, your unconscious mind will resist your efforts.

The unconscious mind operates on the UN-conscious level which means that your conscious mind is COMPLETELY UN-aware of it's machinations.

Your unconscious mind is not going to knock on your door and openly reveal to you its plans for sabotaging your progress.

Your unconscious mind will seek, crafty, sneaky and ingenious ways to divert you and distract you from your path. These distractions will always seem very rational to you at the time. But, if you have people around you who tell you the truth, they will see that your fears are irrational.

So, in order to achieve major life changes, we need to become aware of our unconscious fears and strategies to sabotage our success.

There is a difference between the shamanic approach of dealing with unconscious resistance and the pop-psychological approach.

Pop psychology wants to intellectually examine the unconscious mind with the theory that if we uncover the unconscious mind, we will know our unconscious patterns and be able to avoid unconscious resistance in the future.

The shamanic approach suggests taking direct action toward your desires first. Then, the unconscious mind will kick in and seek to sabotage our success and the underlying fears and patterns will become apparent.

Once you know the strategy of your unconscious mind, you can thwart the unconscious mind's plan to sabotage you. But, the unconscious mind is also very flexible. When one strategy doesn't work, it will often switch gears and use another approach you don't see coming.

This is why it is so important to have a teacher or counselor who can objectively point out your irrational, unconscious fears to you. This is probably the most important service I offer my students and clients. I help them uncover the ingenious schemes of their unconscious mind.

The most powerful way to overcome unconscious resistance and change the underlying sabotaging patterns is to take "contrary action."

Contrary action means that when your fears and self sabotaging drama kicks in, you take CONTRARY ACTION. When your fears tell you to stop, you do the opposite, regardless of how you feel.

I'll give you an example of a powerful method to overcome unconscious resistance. Think of someone you know or have known who is the most unhappy, unsuccessful person you know. Family members or childhood friends are good for this because you have known and watched them for a long time.

More than likely, you will be able to see how this person sabotages their own happiness. They may complain about being a victim of circumstances, but you will most likely be able to see that their misery is entirely of their own making.

They, however, will vehemently defend their resistance, "You don't understand, I can't leave my abusive boyfriend, he's paying my medical bills." Even though it is their abusive boyfriend who is sending them to the hospital most of the time. They have all kinds of irrational excuses for staying miserable.

It's easy for us to see when others are doing this, but it is very difficult to see when we are doing this in our own lives. That's because the unconscious mind wants to stay hidden. If you knew what the unconscious mind was doing, you wouldn't listen to it. So, it stays hidden and concocts ingenious methods to fool us into staying stuck.

This is the power of UN-conscious resistance. We are not consciously aware of how we are seeking to stay miserable.

So, back to our method to overcoming our unconscious fears… Bring to mind this sad, unsuccessful person that you know. They are your best teacher when it comes to overcoming your unconscious fears.

Whenever you are confused, in doubt or whenever you find yourself operating from fear, anger or any other fear based emotion, ask yourself "What would so-and-so do?" Then immediately do the exact opposite.

Virtually every time, you will see that so-and-so always takes fearful actions that prevent them from making positive changes in their lives…

I have a "so-and-so" in my life. I'll call him 'Carl.' This is a man I have known my whole life. He is easily the most unhappy, miserable and unsuccessful person I have ever known.

He wasn't always this way. As a kid, he was very popular. He was the fearless, tough guy on the block that all the other kids wanted to emulate. He was fearless, strong and full of self-confidence.

He was kind of a bully at times, but so are a lot of alpha male types. From the looks of it, as a kid, if he applied himself in life, he was assured to be a success at whatever he put his mind to.

Fast forward to today. Carl is broke, homeless, sick and miserable. He has no family, friends, job or future. It is amazing that he is still alive. He somehow manages to stay alive despite how miserable his life is.

He currently suffers from a debilitating, progressive illness that causes him severe pain. His doctors have told him that his illness is a result of emotional stress, yet he adamantly refuses to seek professional counseling to relieve his stress.

Carl, because of the nature of his illness, could easily qualify for public assistance, but he refuses to even apply. I believe he does this because, on an unconscious level, he prefers to be a victim. He likes to complain. So, the more tragic his life is, the easier it is for him to complain about his life.

If you were to meet him, you might feel pity for him as he would tell you a horrible tale of how life had victimized him. He's very good at spinning this tale of woe. But, I have known him his whole life and I have watched him build, brick by brick, his personal prison of misery.

Now, his life is his business. But he is my greatest teacher in how to live a happy, successful life. If Carl's life is a result of his efforts to be miserable, the most logical strategy to a happy life is to do the opposite of what Carl would do.

I know him so well that I know what he would do and say in just about any situation.

So, in order to get the most out of my life, I simply apply his method of living in complete reverse. Carl has unwittingly taught me one of the greatest skills in achieving a happy life. He teaches me how to take "contrary action."

Whenever I am confronted with a frightening situation in my life, whenever I want to hide or feel like a victim, I ask myself, "What would Carl do right now?" And then I do the exact opposite.

It works every time. Whenever I want to hide or feel victimized, I imagine Carl, what he would say and what he would do. I listen to his advice and regardless of how scary it sounds, I do the exact opposite.

Sometimes this is frightening. Sometimes taking Carl's way out of life sounds really good. Sometimes playing the victim feels safe. It sure sounds convincing. But, since I am more afraid of being miserable and sick like Carl, I do the exact opposite regardless of how scary or "impractical" it may seem to me at the time.

This approach, as I said, always, always works. My life always gets better when I do the opposite of Carl. I am so grateful for everything he teaches me.

Now, sometimes it is not easy at all to take contrary action. Sometimes doing things like Carl does sounds very attractive. But, there is one thing I have noticed about Carl, he always finds reasons NOT to take action.

And whenever I am afraid, I want to NOT take action too. And I see the Carl in myself.

Carl and I are exactly alike. We have the same feelings, temperament, inclinations, desires and fears. We were very alike growing up. We even looked alike. The only major difference between Carl and me is that Carl never takes action contrary to his fears. I have managed to take a few actions contrary to my fears, so I have achieved a greater measure of happiness and success.

Carl thinks that is because I got all the breaks in life whereas he was denied everything. But, I was there. I saw how Carl was given a lot of opportunities and he sabotaged all of them.

But to be honest, from my perspective, Carl has more potential than I do. He is stronger than I am in many ways. He has an extremely strong will. He just uses his willpower to sabotage his life. I'm not as strong as Carl, so even though I too have a self sabotaging streak, I'm just not tough enough to be as miserable as Carl is. I couldn't survive living his life.

Having known Carl all my life and having seen firsthand all of Carl's strengths, gifts and abilities, I can see how, if he had simply taken just a few actions toward his desires, even when he was afraid, he would be very successful in life.

The truth is that Carl has worked extremely hard at being a failure. If he had put 10% of the effort he puts into being miserable into taking actions, he would be extremely successful.

So, one of the first things you can do to achieve success is to bring to mind your version of Carl and imagine what he or she would do and then, just do the opposite.

So, unlike the pop psychology approach, I am not suggesting that you try to completely understand your unconscious mind before taking action. That is simply not possible.

Taking action will threaten your unconscious patterns and bring them out of hiding. They will reveal themselves when threatened. And if you continue to TAKE DIRECT ACTION toward your desires regardless of your fears, you will eventually become aware of how your unconscious fears sabotaged you.

But, in the moment, most likely, you will feel afraid and confused. But, when you learn how to take action regardless of how scared, depressed, sick, poor, alone etc., you may feel, you will eventually learn how to identify and overcome your unconscious resistance when it raises its head.

And this is probably most important. It is never too late to take action and turn things around. It may feel impossible, especially if, like Carl, you have invested a lot of time and energy into sabotaging yourself.

But, the great thing about taking contrary action or doing the opposite of Carl is you don't have to think about it or "feel" ready. Just do the opposite of Carl, take the action regardless of how you feel and watch your life change! So, stop thinking about it and just DO IT!

Thanks, Carl for being my greatest teacher, I owe all my success to you!

The Purpose of Unconscious Resistance

So, forgive me if I have given the impression that the unconscious mind is the devil. It isn't.

The unconscious mind is trying very hard to help us. But, without the guidance of the superconscious mind, the unconscious mind can come to some irrational conclusions about what is best for us.

The reason why the unconscious mind is sometimes so persistent about sabotaging our success is because it believes that it is protecting us from danger.

As children, when we encounter frightening situations, our unconscious minds create psychological patterns in an attempt to prevent us from being harmed in the future. But often times, the unconscious mind makes incorrect assumptions about what is harmful to us.

Let me give you an example in my own life. For much of my adult life, I have struggled with being a writer and a teacher. I have struggled with my own success and prosperity.

On a conscious level, I was working extremely hard to be successful, but no matter how hard I tried, it seemed that I just couldn't make anything happen.

It has taken years of self-examination and work in this area to understand the false assumptions that my unconscious mind made when I was a kid.

My false UN-conscious assumption was this:

My parents will love me only if I am <u>unsuccessful</u>.

I was totally unaware of this psychological pattern in my unconscious mind. And even though I would try extremely hard to become successful, my unconscious mind would sabotage my success at every turn.

My unconscious mind was sabotaging my success because it believed that success would be harmful to me. My unconscious mind was mistakenly trying to protect me from being rejected.

The way this happened was that my Father (rest his soul) was an extremely successful physicist. But he had grown up in a less than supportive home as a kid. So, he was very insecure about himself. Whenever I would achieve something in school, he would find ways to dismiss my accomplishments.

He would even criticize me and tell how I was nowhere near as successful as he was at my age etc,... But, when I was a mediocre student, I got a lot more positive attention from my father.

Even though my dad would talk about how important it was for me to be successful in school, the reality was that when I was successful my dad would withhold love and approval. And if I was a success, he would criticize me.

So, my unconscious mind learned the real emotional communication which was, "If you want my love and approval, you need to be a mediocre person and avoid success."

So, every time in adulthood, when I was approaching success in a field, my unconscious mind would kick in and do an end run around my conscious mind and find ways to sabotage my success.

The main way my unconscious mind would sabotage my success was to prevent me from taking action toward my dreams.

So, now even when I am scared to take action, I do it anyway, regardless of whatever feelings I may have to the contrary.

So, the bottom line here is that your unconscious mind is trying to protect you. The only way, in my experience to overcome the unconscious mind is by taking action and then talking with someone about the fears and feelings that come up.

So, while I am on the subject, let's look at some of the most common symptoms of unconscious resistance:

Lethargy, Laziness, Sadness, Depression, Anger, Resentment, Guilt, Victim Mentality, Obsessions, Drama, Chaos, Loneliness, Addictions, Isolation,

Oversleeping, Insomnia, Fear, Panic, Being Too Busy, Conspiracy Thinking, Poverty, Headaches...

And here is one of the biggest modern symptoms of unconscious resistance.... **Physical Illnesses**.

Here are a few common Resistance Illnesses:
Migraines, Tendonitis, Indigestion, Backaches, Joint Pain, Arthritis, Fibromyalgia, Carpal Tunnel Syndrome, Immune Disorders, High Blood Pressure, Cancer
the list goes on...

(For those suffering from chronic illnesses, I recommend my book, "The Shamanic Secret To Healing Cancer." Even if you are not a cancer sufferer, the healing protocol in that book will apply to any resistance illness.)

Now, look back at your life and ask yourself if ANY of these symptoms or illnesses prevented you from taking action toward your deepest desires.

If so, I am here to tell you that none of these circumstances no matter how challenging, has the power to prevent you from taking continuous action toward your desires.

And, in my experience, the only way to permanently eradicate these symptoms is by taking continuous actions towards your desires.

Take the example of my friend's dad who cured himself of Parkinson's disease by finally allowing himself to be loved and enjoy his life...

Sounds simplistic, but, in my experience it is true. Consistently and fearlessly go after your deepest desires and you can overcome any obstacles.

Conclusion

This little book is just the beginning to this exciting journey of creating your perfect life.

Let's try to sum up the steps to achieving your perfect life:

1) Remember being happy is the main reason you were born. Your highest responsibility to the Universe is to make yourself happy FIRST.
2) In order for the Secret Shamanic Commandment to work, you must obey your deepest desires without compromise.
3) Imagine what you would do if you lived in a perfect fantasy world where you can be and do ANYTHING you want and then take direct and continuous action to achieve it.
4) Be prepared for your UN-conscious mind to try and sabotage your success by diverting you from your goal.
5) Remember your 'Carl.' Ask yourself what Carl would do and then do the exact opposite REGARDLESS of how you feel.
6) If needed, be sure to have a mentor or counselor on your side to help keep you committed to your dream.
7) Be available to share this path with anyone who comes along and asks about your success.

The most important thing to remember is that creating your perfect life is already naturally programmed into your soul.

If you can listen to your Soul, you will always be guided to your highest destiny.

For those with persistent challenges in creating your perfect life, I strongly suggest working with an objective, encouraging professional to help you achieve your desires.

For those wishing personalized consultations, please contact me via my website:
ThunderShamanism.com

or email me at:
info@thundershamanism.com

Thanks for taking the time to read this little book.
Peace and Success,
Michael William Denney

Made in the USA
Monee, IL
26 July 2023